Remind children of the lilac level story they read called 'Pop!' Explain that this is a play version of that story.

Check the children understand that a play means that they perform the parts of the different characters.

Pop! A Play

Kangaroo has lots of balloons. Will Hedgehog get one?

OBJECTIVE
To become aware of character and dialogue

ISBN 0-433-02683-9
9 780433 026839

YELLOW LEVEL

Walkthrough

This is the back cover.

Let's read the blurb together.

Will Hedgehog get a balloon?

What might happen to Hedgehog's balloon?

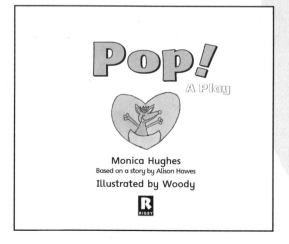

Monica Hughes
Based on a story by Alison Hawes
Illustrated by Woody

Walkthrough

Let's re-read the title: 'Pop! A Play'

Look at the picture.

Why do you think the kangaroo is wearing a party hat?

Look at the author's name. It says Monica Hughes is the author of the play but that the play is based on a story written by Alison Hawes.

1

Walkthrough

This book is written as a play.

Do you know what a play is?

Why do you think there are faces on these balloons?

Yes, these are the characters in the play.

Let's read their names.

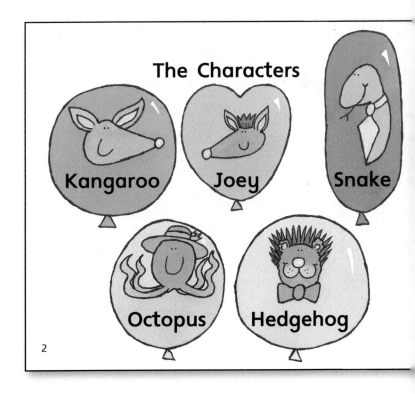

The Characters

Kangaroo   Joey   Snake

Octopus   Hedgehog

2

👁 **Observe and Prompt**

Read the names of the characters with the children.

Walkthrough

On each page, a picture and the name of the character appears beside the words that character says.

On this page, it is Kangaroo who is talking. (Point to picture of Kangaroo and Kangaroo's name.)

What does Kangaroo say?

Let's re-read together what Kangaroo says.

 Kangaroo:
Look! I have some balloons.

3

 Observe and Prompt

Check the children do not read the name of the character, only the words the character speaks.

If necessary, prompt children to read only the words the character speaks.

Walkthrough

Look at the right-hand page.

Who is Kangaroo giving the blue balloon to?

Snake looks pleased.

Now look at the left-hand page.

Who is speaking on this page? Use the little pictures to help you.

 Kangaroo:
The blue balloon is for you.

 Snake:
Thank you.
I like my blue balloon!

4

 Observe and Prompt

Observe one-to-one correspondence.

If a child misses out 'blue', ask him/her to look at the picture to see what colour the balloon is, then ask to re-read the sentence, carefully finger-pointing to each word.

What do you think the Kangaroo says?

What do you think the Snake says?

What do you say when someone gives you something? (*Thank you*)

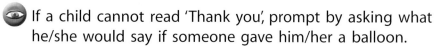 If a child cannot read 'Thank you', prompt by asking what he/she would say if someone gave him/her a balloon.

Walkthrough

Look at the picture on the right-hand page.

Who is Kangaroo giving the little balloons to?

Let's say his name again: 'Octopus'.

Octopus looks pleased. What do you think he is saying?

 Kangaroo:
The little balloons are
for you.

 Octopus:
Thank you.
I like my little balloons!

6

Look at the left-hand page.

Who is speaking?

What do you think Kangaroo is saying?

What do you think Octopus is saying?

👁 Observe and Prompt

Observe one-to-one correspondence.

If a child reads 'small' for 'little', praise the child for thinking about the meaning, but ask child to look at the initial letter and try the word again.

Walkthrough

Now Hedgehog is asking for a balloon.

Say his name again: 'Hedgehog'.

What sort of balloons does Kangaroo
give Hedgehog?

 Hedgehog:
I like balloons, too.
Can I have a balloon?

 Kangaroo:
Yes.
The big balloons are
for you.

8

Do you think it's a good idea for Hedgehog to have a balloon?

What might happen?

![eye icon] **Observe and Prompt**

Observe children reading 'Can I have a balloon?' as a question; if necessary, prompt them to look at the question mark and raise their voice at the end of the line.

Walkthrough

Hedgehog is very pleased with all his balloons.

He says, 'Look at me! Look at all **my** balloons!'

How does Kangaroo feel?

What does she say?

What do you think is about to happen?

 Hedgehog:
Look at me!
Look at all **my** balloons!

 Kangaroo:
Look out!
Look out!

10

 Observe and Prompt

Observe children reading with expression and paying attention to exclamation marks.

Prompt children to add expression when reading, to make Hedgehog sound excited and Kangaroo sound worried.

11

Walkthrough

What has happened here?

Can you see the word 'pop' in the picture?

What do you think Hedgehog is saying?

What do you think Octopus and Snake
are saying?

 Hedgehog:
Oh, no!
All my balloons went **pop!**

 **Octopus and
Snake:**
Oh, no!
All his balloons went **pop!**

12

 Observe and Prompt

Check the children read Hedgehog's lines with expression.

If child cannot read 'all', supply it.

Walkthrough

What is Joey doing?

What do you think he said?

Isn't Joey kind?

 Joey:
Look! You can have my balloon.

14

 Observe and Prompt

Observe one-to-one correspondence.

Walkthrough

How does Hedgehog feel now?

How can you tell?

What do you think Hedgehog is saying to Joey?

Hedgehog:
Thank you! Thank you!
Thank you!

16

Observe and Prompt

Check the children read Hedgehog's words with expression.